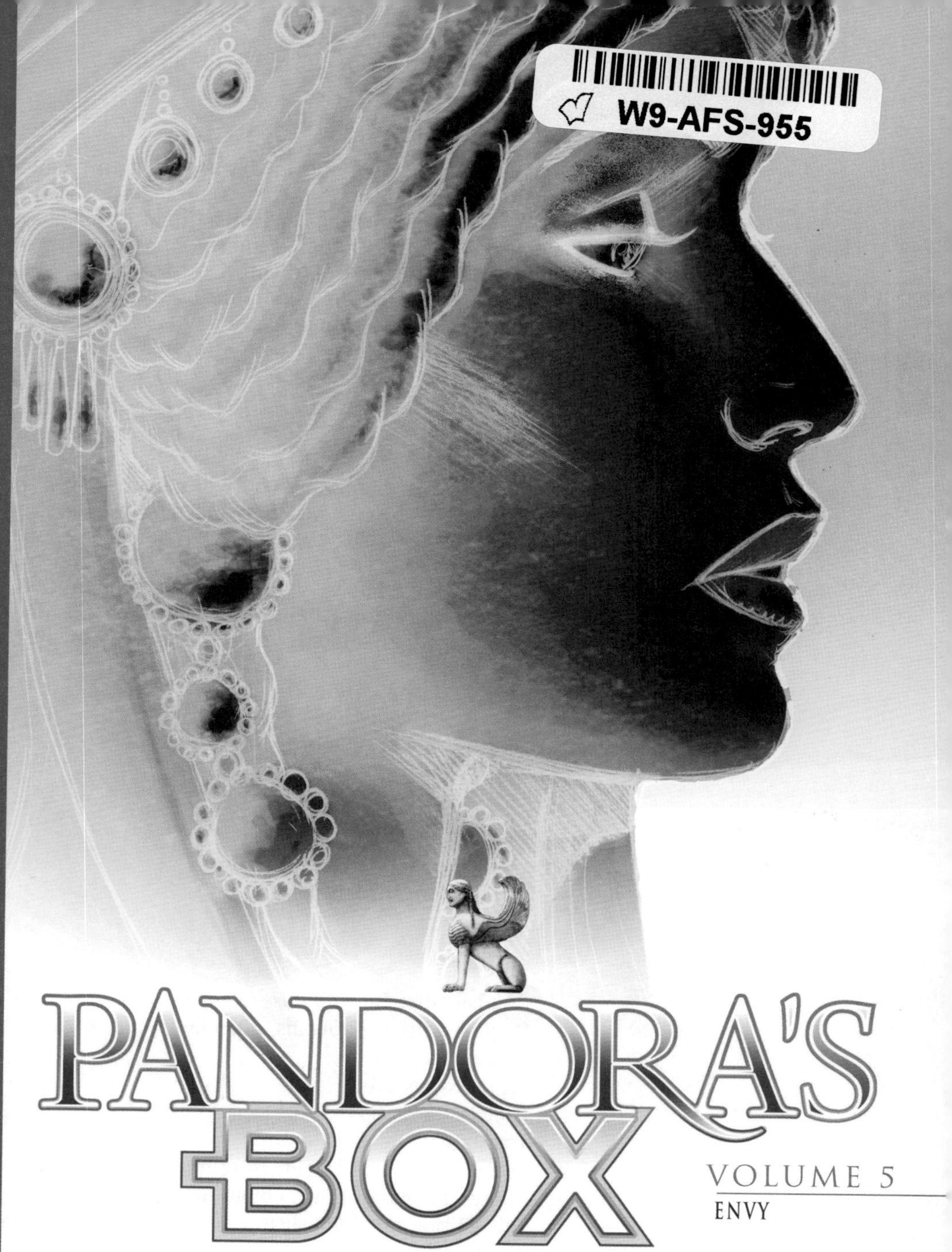

PANDORA'S BOX

VOLUME 5

ENVY

Drawing
ALAIN HENRIET

Script
ALCANTE

Colour work
USAGI

Prometheus

One of the Titans, and initiator of human civilisation. Moved by the plight of men—who, at first, were mere toys of the gods—he rebelled against the Olympians. With the help of Athena, daughter of Zeus, he snuck into the gods' demesne and stole the sacred fire, offering it to men so they could throw off the divine shackles. Zeus had Hephaestus, the lame god, capture him. He was then bound to Mount Caucasus, where every day an eagle would come and eat his liver, and every night it would grow back...

Pandora's Box

Of Pride, like Narcissus, you will pay the heavy price.
Of Sloth, like Paris, you will succumb to the slow venom.
Of Gluttony, like Theseus, you will know the foul torment.
Of Lust, like Orpheus, you will bite the bitter fruit.
Of Greed, like Midas, you will learn the hard law.
Of Envy, like Prometheus, you will suffer the eternal punishment.
Of Wrath, like Pandora, you will be the fatal instrument.

Finally, at the very end,
Your soul seven times destroyed,
Only hope will remain,
To live and rise again.

Thus spoke the Oracle
When the box was opened
And its savage spice
Into the world had spread.

Original title: Pandora Box – L'envie

Translator: Jerome Saincantin
Lettering and text layout: Imadjinn
Printed in Spain by Just Colour Graphic
This edition first published in Great Britain in 2011 by
Cinebook Ltd
56 Beech Avenue
Canterbury, Kent
CT4 7TA
www.cinebook.com
A CIP catalogue record for this book
is available from the British Library
ISBN 978-1-84918-079-5

PROVIDENCE, RHODE ISLAND, UNITED STATES...
A DAY JUST LIKE ANY OTHER, IN THE NEAR FUTURE...
EARER THAN OU MIGHT THINK!
AHH!
SAME DREAM AGAIN?
YEAH...
WHAT ABOUT YOU? SLEPT WELL?
MMM HMM... I DREAMED OF THE GRAND CANYON... DO YOU THINK WE'LL EVER GO THERE?
I DON'T KNOW... I THINK THAT GREAT JOURNEYS AREN'T REALLY FOR THE LIKES OF US... COME ON, WE'VE GOT TO GO NOW...

HELLO...? HELLO...? DAMMIT, WE GOT CUT OFF!

DRRIIIIIINNG!
EXPLOSION INSIDE A BUILDING! THIS IS BI GUYS. MOVE IT!!!

WWOEE WOOEE WOOE

YOU GO, MY BOYS...

... AND GOD BE WITH YOU!!
LET US READ FROM EXODUS, CHAPTER 20, VERSE 17...
YOU SHALL NOT COV YOUR NEIGHBOUR'S HOUSE. YOU SHALL NOT COVET YOUR NEIGHBOUR'S WIF OR HIS MALE OR FEMALE SERVANT, HIS OX OR DONKEY, OR ANYTHING THAT BELONGS TO YOUR NEIGHBOUR. AND N

... LET US PRAISE...
... THE ALMIGHTY...
THE ATTORNEY GENERAL CALLED. HE ASKED IF IT WOULD BE POSSIBLE TO POSTPONE TOMORROW'S MEETING...
I'LL CALL HIM IN A LITTLE WHILE. EALLY LIKE THAT DRESS, SS CHAMBERLAIN, EVEN F IT'S STILL TOO TAME FOR MY TASTE...
MORE PEOPLE DEMONSTRATING... CAN YOU BELIEVE THERE'S A NATIONWIDE PROTEST TAKING PLACE TODAY? WHAT ON EARTH DO THEY WANT, ANYWAY?
WELL... A BETTER LIFE, MAYBE?

A BETTER LIFE...?
WHAT A STRANGE NOTION...
YOU'RE NOT LIKE EVERYONE ELSE... TODAY, YOUR ADVENTURE BEGINS. WHEN THE STORY IS OVER, GIRL, YOUR FACE WILL HAVE CHANGED BUT YOUR SOUL WILL REMAIN THE SAME. AS FOR YOU, MY BOY, IT WILL BE THE OPPOSITE...
A LITTLE LATER...
HI, TIBOR. HOW ARE YOU DOING?
SAME AS ALWAYS, BOSS; SAME AS ALWAYS.

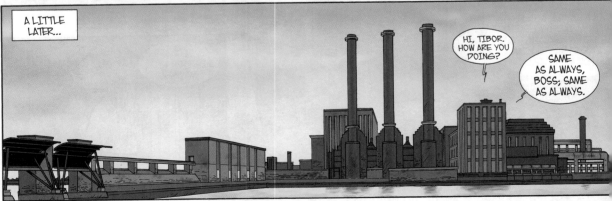

TIBOR, MAY I HAVE A WORD?

LIAM? ER, YES, OF COURSE. GO AHEAD...

LISTEN, IT CAN'T GO ON LIKE THIS. MOST OF THE GUYS HAVE HAD ENOUGH. THEY TREAT US LIKE CRAP ...

THERE HAVE ALREADY BEEN A LOT OF LAYOFFS, AND THE SCUTTLEBUTT SAYS IT'S ONLY THE BEGINNING. IT'S BECOMING UNBEARABLE. WE HAVE TO WORK EXTRA HOURS ALL THE TIME, AND THE CONDITIONS ARE HORRIBLE.
I KNOW ALL THAT, LIAM. IT'S HARD FOR EVERYONE.

BUT WE DON'T REALLY HAVE A CHOICE, BUDDY!
BULLSHIT! OF COURSE WE HAVE A CHOICE! STOP SAYING THAT!

WE DON'T EVEN KNOW WHAT THE PARTS WE MAKE ARE FOR; SAFETY AND HYGIENE ARE GETTING WORSE EVERY DAY; I EVEN SAW SOME RATS AROU HERE. AND DON'T EVEN GET ME STARTED ON OUR MISERABLE PAYCHEQUE ME AND MY WIFE, WE CAN'T MAKE ENDS MEET ANYMORE!

LISTEN, CALM DOWN...
ANYTIME IT GETS CHEAPER FOR THEM TO REPLACE A GUY WITH A MACHINE, THEY GO AHEAD—AND ALL YOU CAN TELL ME IS THAT WE DON'T HAVE A CHOICE?!
CAUCASIUS

THERE ARE A LOT OF GUYS HERE WHO'D BE READY TO GO ON STRIKE IF YOU WERE WITH US. YOU KNOW YOU'VE GOT A LOT OF INFLUENCE OVER THEM... YOU'RE THE ONLY ONE THEY LISTEN TO...
NO, LIAM. IT'S A BAD IDEA.

MANAGEMENT IS DOING THEIR BEST, BUT GLOBAL COMPETITION IS WHAT IT IS. IF WE DON'T CUT COSTS, WE'LL BE HEADING STRAIGHT FOR BANKRUPTCY. IT'S AS SIMPLE AS THAT. WE'D ALL LOSE OUR JOBS!!! AND YOU KNOW WHAT THAT MEANS, LOSING YOUR JOB NOWADAYS...?
WITHOUT YOU, THE GUYS WON'T FOLLOW... SO, ARE YOU WITH US OR NOT...?
6.

NO...

TIBOR, WE'VE GOT A PROBLEM IN THE HOLDING TANK. COME TAKE A LOOK...
OH, NO. NOT ANOTHER LEAK...
YEAH, THERE'S WATER EVERYWHERE.
BLASTED MACHINE... EVA, CAN YOU COME WITH US? YOU KNOW THAT THING BETTER THAN ANYONE.
I TOLD THEM A HUNDRED TIMES THAT WE HAD TO CHANGE THE SEAL, DAMMIT! IT'S NO WONDER IT FINALLY GAVE WAY ENTIRELY!
WATCH...
AHHHH!!

OK, IT'S TURNED OFF NOW!
YOU ALL RIGHT? DAMN, YOU COULD HAVE BEEN KILLED!
WE'RE FINE, WE'RE OK... DON'T WORRY...
BOSTON UNIVERSITY
SO, WHO CAN TELL ME THE NINE DOMAINS OF INTELLIGENCE AS DESCRIBED IN GARDNER'S EXTENDED MODEL? YES, YOU...?
LOGICAL-MATHEMATICAL, LINGUISTIC, MUSICAL, BODILY-KINESTHETIC, SPATIAL, INTERPERSONAL, INTRAPERSONAL, NATURALISTIC, AND... AND...
YOU FORGOT ONE. I'LL GIVE YOU THE ANSWER NEXT TIME. YOU MAY GO.
BEEEP BEEEP
IS IT ABOUT SYNAPSE'S BID?
YOUR BID MADE IT INTO THE FINAL STAGE OF SELECTION, YES, ALONG WITH FOUR OTHERS. BUT THAT'S NOT WHY I'M CALLING...

A FEW HOURS LATER...
EVEN IF YOU LOOK PERFECTLY FINE, I'D RATHER NOT TAKE ANY CHANCES WITH YOUR HEALTH.

AT'S WHY I HAD THESE PEOPLE OM THE MEDICAL DEPARTMENT OME OVER. THEY'RE GOING TO AMINE YOU... IVAN, LET'S START TH YOU. PLEASE GO INTO THE XT ROOM.

BILL, COME WITH ME. MIKE, YOU STAY WITH THEM.

SYNAPSE

SYNAPSE

AHHHHH!

REMAIN SEATED!
WHAT...?!

I SAID, DON'T MOVE!!

WHAT KIND OF CARD IS THAT? GET OUT OF MY WAY!
IVAN, ARE YOU OK!?!
HEY!?
WHAT THE...?!?
THE PROMEMS AREN'T WORKING WE CAN'T LET THEM LEAVE!
AHHH!!

COME ON! LET'S GET OUT OF HERE!

HELP! CALL THE POLICE!!

BOSS, THEY'RE TRYING TO KILL US!?!

?!

HE'S LOCKING US IN!!

HERE!

DID YOU EVER CONSIDER THE CONSEQUENCES OF YOUR ACTIONS? YOU GAVE ME LIFE AND THEN YOU LEFT ME TO DIE... WHO AM I??

I DON'T KNOW...

YES?
I NEED YOU TO CATCH SOME RUNAWAYS. THEY'RE WORTH SEVERAL MILLION DOLLARS...
I'M TELLING YOU THEY TRIED TO KILL US!!
CALM DOWN. YOU'RE SAFE NOW. SIT DOWN AND WAIT FOR YOUR TURN, SIR.

DANGEROUS!

WE HAVE TO CALL OUR NEIGHBOURS!
WHAT THE HELL IS THIS ALL ABOUT?
NYPD POLICE

WHAT'S GOING ON? SOME COPS CAME AND ASKED ME SOME QUESTIONS ABOUT YOU!! THEY'RE TALKING ABOUT A MURDER... HELLO? HELLO?

CRAP!

WHAT ON EARTH ARE YOU HOPING TO FIND, ANYWAY?!?
CYBERCAFE
24/7

welcome to SYNAPSE
THIS!

SYNAPSE SPECIALISES IN THE USE OF CERTAIN TOOLS (PYTHON, XML, PLONE...) AND TECHNIQUES (ENGINEERING, SOFTWARE, STATISTICS, LOGIC...) TO APPLY THEM TO ADVANCED COMPUTER SCIENCE (IMPLEMENTATION OF INTELLIGENT AGENTS, ANALYSIS OF NATURAL LANGUAGE, SIMULATION, DATA ANALYSIS, SCIENTIFIC CALCULATIONS...).

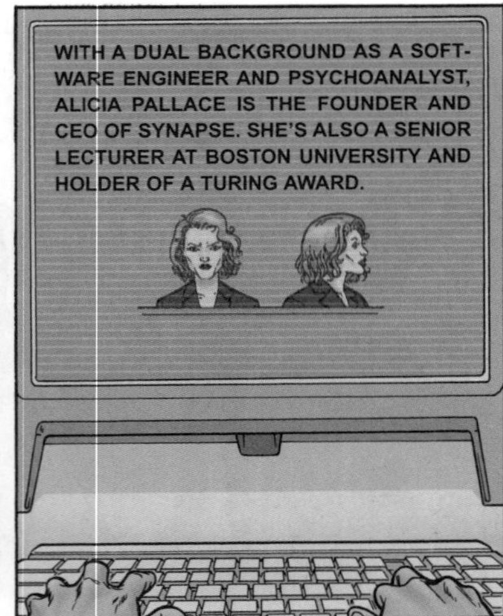

WITH A DUAL BACKGROUND AS A SOFTWARE ENGINEER AND PSYCHOANALYST, ALICIA PALLACE IS THE FOUNDER AND CEO OF SYNAPSE. SHE'S ALSO A SENIOR LECTURER AT BOSTON UNIVERSITY AND HOLDER OF A TURING AWARD.

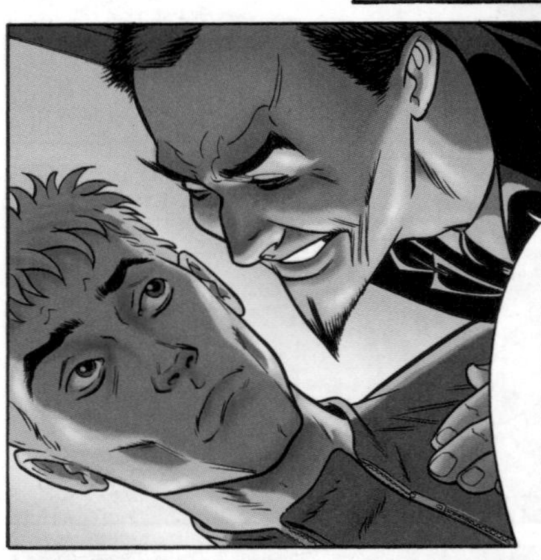

HEY!?

WHAT HAPPENED?
YOU WERE ELECTROCUTED ON THE ASSEMBLY LINE...
OH, YES... I REMEMBER NOW...

WHAT ELSE DO YOU REMEMBER?
NOTHING!

PERFECT...

MISS CHAMBERLAIN, I'M NOT PAYING YOU TO FLIRT DURING OFFICE HOURS!!

I APOLOGISE, MR ROY...

THE SYMBOL OF ENVY IS THE SNAKE...

LIKE A SNAKE, IT WRAPS ITSELF AROUND THE HEART, THE BETTER TO SQUEEZE THE NOURISHING BLOOD OUT OF IT, CUTTING MAN OFF FROM THE SOURCE OF LIFE...

CAST AWAY THAT SIN OR YOU WILL KNOW...

... THE FIRES OF HELL!!

MY DAUGHTER!! SHE'S STILL INSIDE!!

I'M ON IT!!

SOFT LIGHTS; DMITRI SHOSTAKOVICH'S PIANO CONCERTO NO. 2, ALLEGRO, OP. 102. HOT BATH, NICE AND DEEP, WITH ESSENTIAL OILS...

YOU ARE OUT OF MILK. SHOULD I ORDER SOME?
YES, ONE GALLON.

HHHH!!
YOU'RE GOING TO EXPLAIN EVERYTHING NOW, YOU BITCH!

WHAT HAPPENED? WHY DID YOU TRY TO HURT US?
LET GO OF ME!!
NOT UNTIL YOU'VE GIVEN US AN EXPLANATION!

THE POLICE ARE LOOKING FOR YOU. YOU DON'T HAVE A CHANCE OF ESCAPING THEM! TURN YOURSELVES IN AND...

ANSWER THE DAMNED QUESTION!
HEY! TAKE IT EASY!!

DO I HAVE TO REMIND YOU THAT THEY TRIED TO KILL US?!
CALM DOWN, WILL YOU?! I'VE NEVER SEEN YOU LIKE THIS!

USUALLY, SHE'D NEVER HURT A FLY. BUT THE ELECTRIC SHOCK MESSED UP EVERYTHING!!

WHAT... WHAT DOES THAT MEAN?
YOU WOULDN'T BELIEVE ME...

LOOK AT THIS...

IF I WERE THEM, I COULD FIND ALICIA WITH THIS!

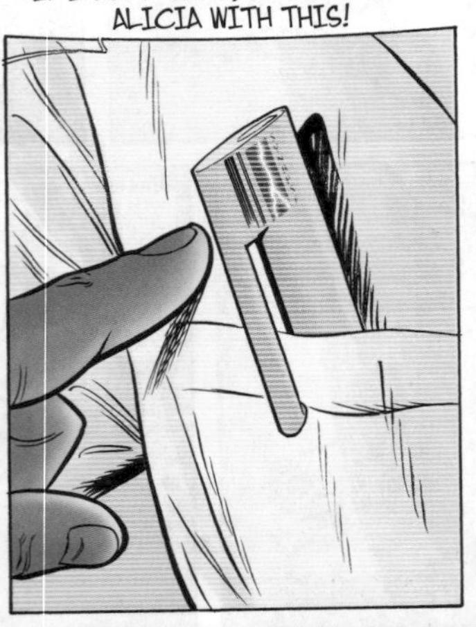

MM... IT SEEMS UNLIKELY, BUT I'LL GIVE HER A CALL JUST IN CASE.

YOU HAVE A CALL FROM CHARLTON ROY. WOULD YOU LIKE TO ANSWER?

WHAT DO I DO?
OK, YOU CAN ANSWER.
IF YOU TRY ANYTHING...
I KNOW...
OK, I'LL TAKE THE CALL.

EVENING.
HAVE YOU FOUND THEM?

NO, NOT YET. BUT BLACKSMITH THINKS THEY COULD IDENTIFY YOU, THANKS TO THE LOGO ON YOUR PEN... SO BE ON YOUR GUARD!

BAH... DON'T WORRY; I'LL WATCH MY BACK. ER... CAN WE DISCUSS DARPA'S CALL FOR BIDS?...
I TOLD YOU ALREADY; SYNAPSE'S BID WAS SHORTLISTED ALONG WITH A FEW OTHERS. WHY ARE YOU SO ANXIOUS? IS SYNAPSE IN FINANCIAL TROUBLE...?

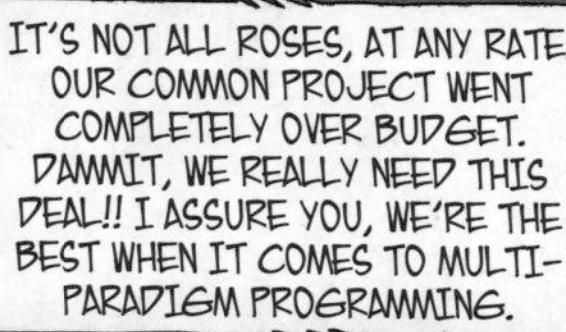
IT'S NOT ALL ROSES, AT ANY RATE. OUR COMMON PROJECT WENT COMPLETELY OVER BUDGET. DAMMIT, WE REALLY NEED THIS DEAL!! I ASSURE YOU, WE'RE THE BEST WHEN IT COMES TO MULTI-PARADIGM PROGRAMMING.

I WON'T BE THE ONLY ONE DECIDING. DON'T COUNT ON ANY FAVOURITISM FROM ME! GOOD NIGHT, ALICIA.

YEAH, I KNOW. NOT ABOUT THIS, NOT ABOUT ANYTHING ELSE...

WHO WAS THAT GUY?!? WHAT DOES HE WANT WITH US??
CHARLTON ROY. HE'S THE DIRECTOR OF DARPA, THE DEFENCE ADVANCED RESEARCH PROJECTS AGENCY. WITH AN ANNUAL BUDGET OF OVER THREE BILLION DOLLARS...

WHAT DOES THAT HAVE TO DO WITH US...?

SHE SEEMED NERVOUS... PLAY THE RECORDING OF THE CONVERSATION AGAIN!

STOP! PAUSE THE RECORDING, NOW!

ARE YOU CRAZY?!? STOP IT!!
SHE'S PLAYING US FOR FOOLS!
YOU REALLY WANT TO KNOW EVERYTHING?... FINE.

A FEW YEARS AGO, A TOP-SECRET PROJECT WAS LAUNCHED, KICK-STARTED BY DARPA. ROY IS THE OVERALL COORDINATOR; ASIDE FROM HIM, ALMOST NO ONE KNOWS THE ULTIMATE GOAL OF THE PROJECT... SYNAPSE IS INVOLVED IN SOME ASPECTS OF THE PROJECT, ALONG WITH OTHER START-UPS AND SEVERAL HEAVYWEIGHTS.

THE PURPOSE OF THE PROJECT IS TO BUILD ANDROIDS—HIGHLY SOPHISTICATED ROBOTS, IF YOU WILL. THE BUDGET IS ASTRONOMICAL, BUT THE POTENTIAL APPLICATIONS ARE JUST AS HUGE.
I STILL DON'T SEE HOW THIS CONCERNS US?!?

YOUR NAME IS TIBOR MEGGONDOLT; SHE'S EVA ADOMANY. YOU BOTH EMIGRATED FROM EASTERN EUROPE. EVA'S PARENTS ARE DEAD; TIBOR NO LONGER SPEAKS TO HIS. PEOPLE ARE SOMETIMES SURPRISED AT HOW COLD YOUR HANDS ARE, AND CELL PHONES TEND TO MALFUNCTION WHEN YOU'RE AROUND.

IN THE PAST YEAR, YOU HAVEN' GONE MORE THAN 20 MILES FROM YOUR HOUSE. EVA OFTE DREAMS ABOUT THE GRAND CANYON... IN THE PAST YEAR, YOU'VE NEVER BEEN SICK, NEVER GONE TO THE DOCTOR
HOW... HOW DO YOU KNOW ALL THIS?

BECAUSE I DESIGNED YOU... YOU'RE THE FIRS ANDROIDS CREATED B THE PROJECT...

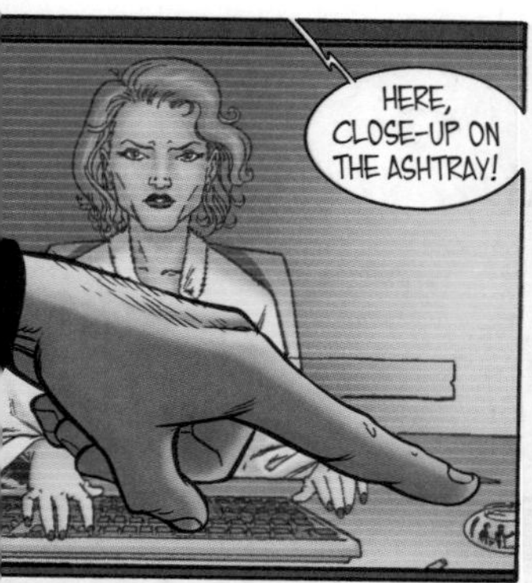
HERE, CLOSE-UP ON THE ASHTRAY!

DAMMIT!
WE FOUND THEM! READY THREE CHOPPERS, EIGHT-MAN SQUAD TO EACH BIRD. ISSUE EACH MAN A PULSE GUN!! WE'LL BE RIGHT THERE!

STOP SCREWING WITH US, DAMMIT!!
THIS IS COMPLETE NONSENSE. I HAVE A FAMILY, PARENTS...

NO, YOU DON'T HAVE PARENTS. THEY'RE FAKE MEMORIES. AS A MATTER OF FACT, YOU WERE IMPLANTED WITH MEMORIES OF SERIOUS PROBLEMS WITH THEM TO MAKE SURE YOU'D NEVER WANT TO CONTACT THEM. THAT'S THE SAME REASON EVA'S IMAGINARY PARENTS ARE SUPPOSED TO BE DEAD...

CALL YOUR PARENTS, RIGHT NOW!!
NO WAY. YOU KNOW I SWORE NEVER TO TALK TO THEM AGAIN AFTER WHAT THEY DID TO ME!

HE WON'T DO IT. IT'S A CONSTRAINT HARD-CODED ONTO HIS MEMORY DRIVE.
SHUT UP! CALL INTERNATIONAL DIRECTORY INFORMATION! I WANT THEIR NUMBER!

21.

I'M SORRY, MA'AM. THERE'S NOBODY BY THAT NAME IN BUDAPEST...
THEY MUST HAVE MOVED AWAY, THEN...

NO. THERE'S NEVER BEEN ANYONE BY THAT NAME IN OUR FILES, MA'AM...

BUT WE'RE MADE OF FLESH AND BONE!?!
NO. YOUR "SKIN" IS MADE OF BIOTECH TISSUE. IT'S A MIX OF ORGANIC AND INTELLIGENT INORGANIC MATTERS. THEY'RE "ALIVE" IN THE SENSE THAT THEY MIMIC ORGANIC FLESH BY REPAIRING THEIR GRADUAL WEAR AND TEAR, THANKS TO NANOTECHNOLOGY. AS FOR YOUR "BONES," THEY'RE ALSO MADE OF ADVANCED COMPOSITES AND SUPPORT ARTIFICIAL MUSCLES MADE OF FIBRES THAT CONTRACT UNDER ELECTRICAL IMPULSES...

WHAT'S THE DEAL WITH THE COLD HANDS?
A SIMPLE QUESTION OF CONSERVING THE ENERGY YOU NEED TO FUNCTION. BRINGING YOUR BODY TEMPERATURE TO 98.6° F SIMPLY USED TOO MUCH POWER...

SO WHAT THE HELL HAPPENED, THEN?
THE ELECTRIC SHOCK DAMAGED YOUR TRANSCEIVERS. WE NOTICED THAT AND CAME TO REPAIR THEM. WHAT WE DIDN'T KNOW WAS THAT YOUR WRITABLE MEMORIE WERE HIT TOO... YOUR CONSTRAINTS WERE FRIED!

WHAT'S THIS ABOUT CONSTRAINTS? YOU'RE NOT MAKING ANY SENSE TO US!!

THE ARTIFICIAL INTELLIGENCE THAT ANIMATES YOU IS IN THREE PARTS. THERE'S THE HARDWARE, WHICH IS COMMON TO ALL ANDROIDS. IT DETERMINES EVERYTHING THAT DEALS WITH THE MECHANICAL ASPECTS OF THE UNIT: LOCOMOTION, BASIC REASONING AND SKILLS—SPEAKING, EATING—AND ITS INSTINCTIVE BEHAVIOUR—AVOIDING DANGER AND SO ON... THIS IS HARD-CODED SOFTWARE THAT CAN'T BE MODIFIED.

THE "DRIVE" MEMORY CONTAINS WHAT CONSTITUTES THE ANDROID'S PERSONALITY: ITS INDIVIDUAL SKILLS, ITS "PAST" —IMPLANTED MEMORIES—TO WHICH ARE ADDED ACTUAL EXPERIENCES—REAL MEMORIES. THESE ARE MERE DATA STRINGS. IF NEED BE, THAT MEMORY CAN BE ERASED AND REPLACED BY ANOTHER, WHICH MEANS IN ESSENCE THAT AN ANDROID'S PERSONALITY CAN CHANGE COMPLETELY.

FINALLY, THE "WRITABLE" MEMORY CONTAINS THE PHYSICAL CONSTRAINTS—THE ANDROID CAN'T LEAVE A CERTAIN GEOGRAPHIC ZONE—AND BEHAVIOURAL CONSTRAINTS—FOR EXAMPLE, "AN ANDROID CANNOT HURT A HUMAN BEING." SHOULD THE NEED ARISE, THAT WRITABLE MEMORY CAN BE REMOTELY MODIFIED USING BLUETOOTH TECHNOLOGY. SUCH DATA TRANSMISSION CAN INTERFERE WITH CELL PHONES.

WHAT HAPPENED WHEN WE GOT SHOCKED?! AND BE CLEAR!!

A ONE-IN-A-MILLION CHAIN OF EVENTS AND CIRCUMSTANCES THAT LED TO YOUR TRANSCEIVER FRYING AND YOUR WRITABLE MEMORY BEING ERASED. HOWEVER, YOUR DRIVE MEMORY REMAINED INTACT.

THE RESULT BEING THAT NOT ONLY COULDN'T WE LOCATE YOU REMOTELY ANYMORE, BUT ALSO THAT YOUR BEHAVIOUR WAS NO LONGER CHECKED BY ANY OF THE CONSTRAINTS WE'D SET UP—LIKE THE FACT THAT YOU WERE SUPPOSED TO OBEY WHOMEVER HELD THE "PROMEM" CARD. IT WAS ONLY WHEN YOUR FRIEND STARTED SCREAMING THAT WE REALISED YOUR WRITABLE MEMORY HAD BEEN ERASED...

ETA THREE MINUTES! THREE MINUTES!

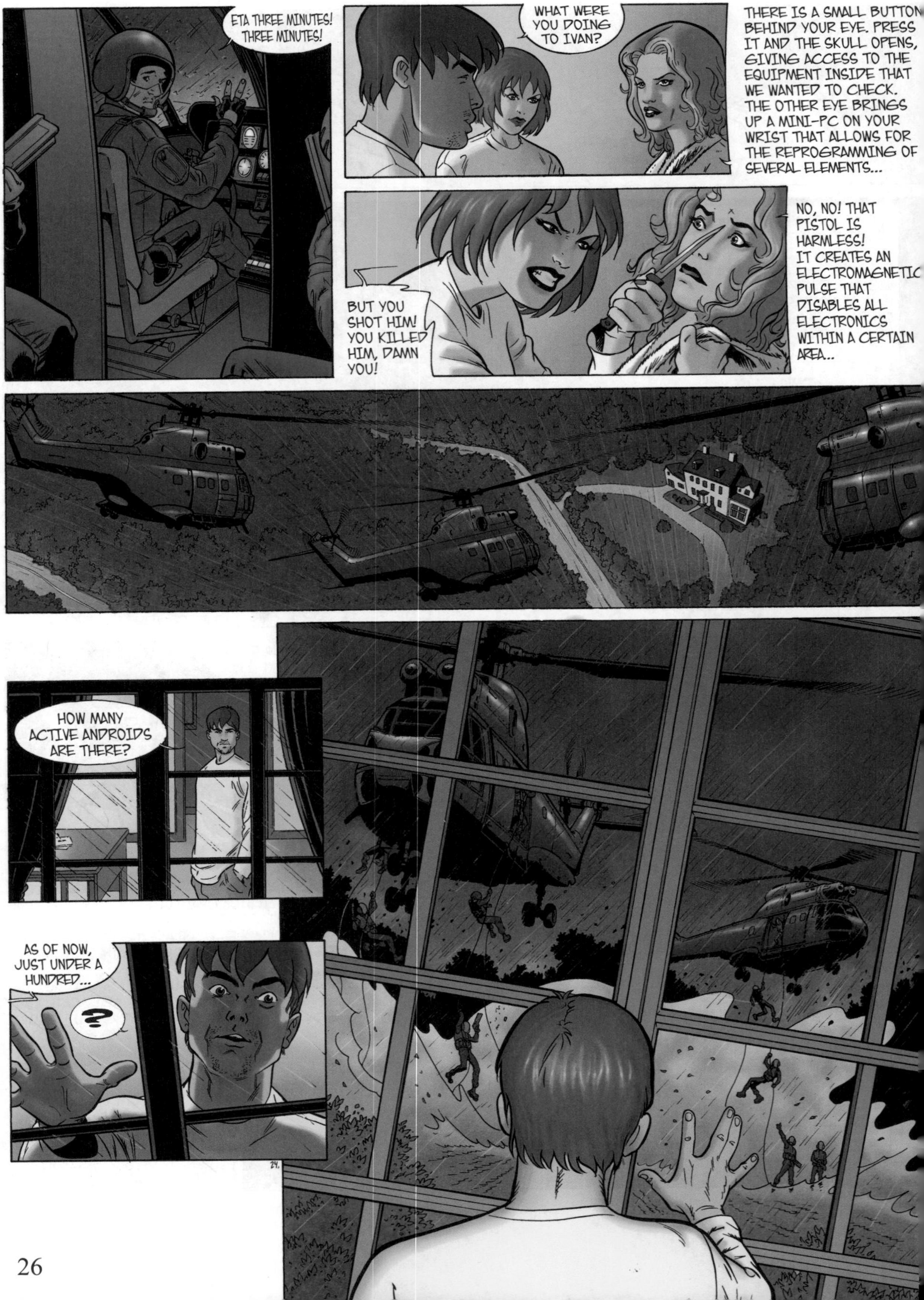

WHAT WERE YOU DOING TO IVAN?
THERE IS A SMALL BUTTON BEHIND YOUR EYE. PRESS IT AND THE SKULL OPENS, GIVING ACCESS TO THE EQUIPMENT INSIDE THAT WE WANTED TO CHECK. THE OTHER EYE BRINGS UP A MINI-PC ON YOUR WRIST THAT ALLOWS FOR THE REPROGRAMMING OF SEVERAL ELEMENTS...

BUT YOU SHOT HIM! YOU KILLED HIM, DAMN YOU!
NO, NO! THAT PISTOL IS HARMLESS! IT CREATES AN ELECTROMAGNETIC PULSE THAT DISABLES ALL ELECTRONICS WITHIN A CERTAIN AREA...

HOW MANY ACTIVE ANDROIDS ARE THERE?

AS OF NOW, JUST UNDER A HUNDRED...

?

VR-R-R-R
R-R-R-R-R-R

THEY'VE GOT PALLACE WITH THEM! AFTER THEM!

CHOPPER 1, GO TO THE OTHER END OF THE TUNNEL; FIVE MEN A EACH EXIT. TRAP THEM INSIDE!
EEEEEEEEEEE
COME ON, MOVE!!

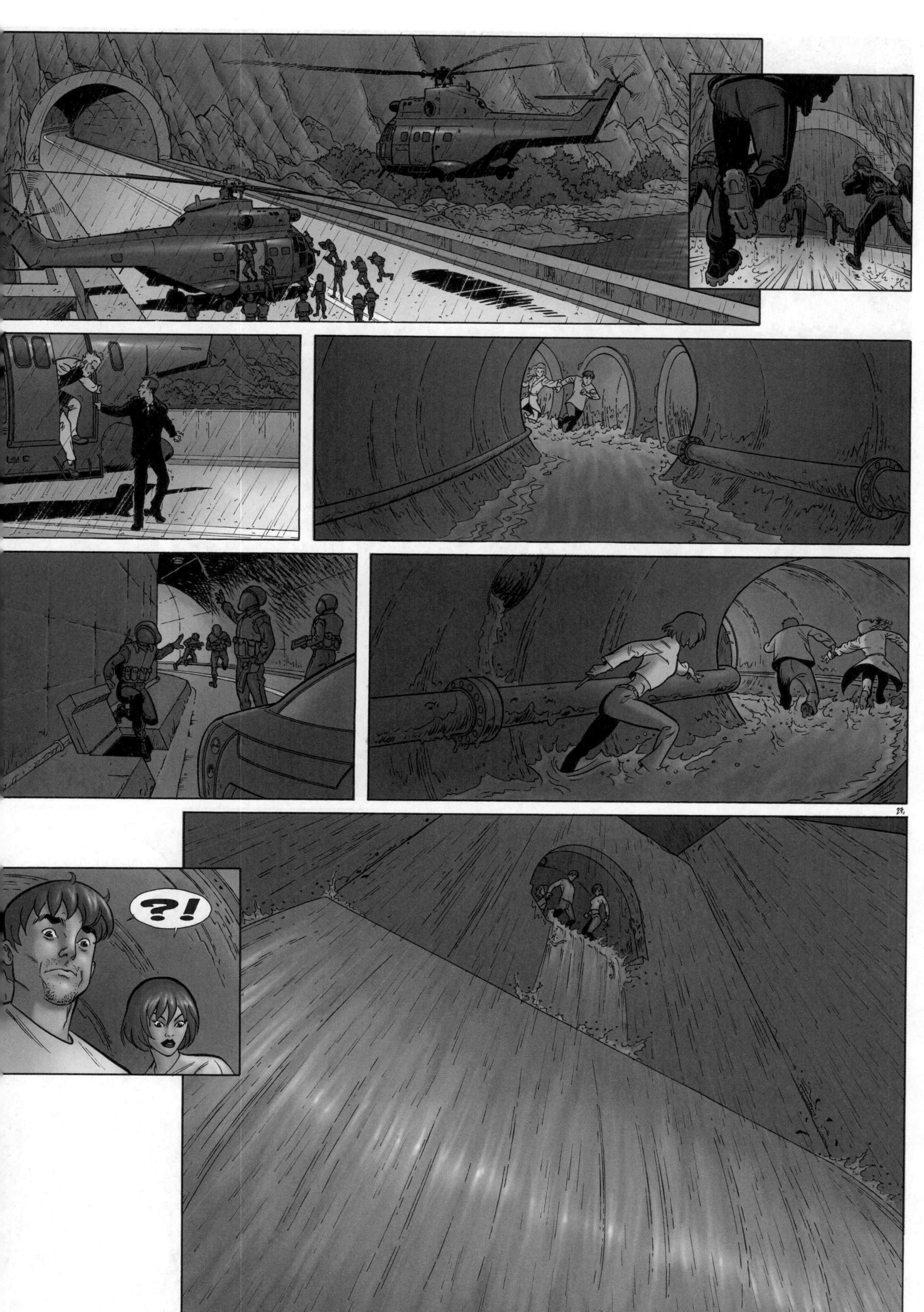

HELP! HELP!
HEY?!

YOU BITCH!

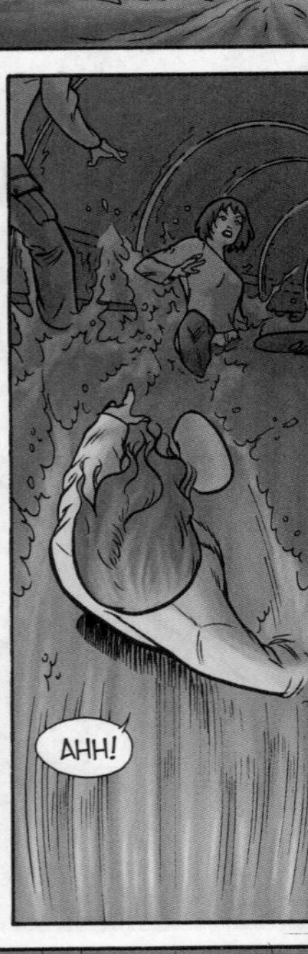
AHH!

AHHHHH, HELP ME!

HURRY UP, DAMMIT, THEY'RE ALMOST HERE!! SCREW HER!!

AHHH!

THERE THEY ARE!

DON'T MOVE!

LEAST THIS WAY YOU'LL HAVE KNOWN A
EW HOURS OF FREEDOM.. HOW DID YOU
LIKE IT?

WHY...?
I WANT TO
KNOW WHY!!

WHY...? BECAUSE OF ENVY, THAT'S WHY! THE
AILMENT OF THE CENTURY, AT THE ROOT OF
EVERYTHING!

THESE DAYS, NOBODY SEEMS ABLE JUST TO ACCEPT THEIR LOT IN LIFE UNLESS IT'S A GOOD ONE. IT'S UNBELIEVABLE. IT'S ALL DEMANDS, STRIKES AND THE DEVIL KNOWS WHAT! AND WE HAVE TO KEEP IT ALL UNDER CONTROL. FOR CRYING OUT LOUD, DO YOU THINK IT'S EASY!?!

SO, WE HAD THE IDEA OF INFIL-TRATING ANDROIDS EVERYWHERE THAT ORDER WAS THREATENED... FIRST, THAT MAKES YOU SPIES FOR US, SINCE EVERYTHING YOU SEE AND HEAR IS RECORDED. IT ALLOWS US TO PICK OUT POTENTIAL TROUBLEMAKERS...

BUT YOU ALSO HAVE A PREVENTATIVE ROLE! YOUR WRITABLE MEMORY ALSO INCLUDED "MORAL" CONSTRAINTS. YOU WERE PROGRAMMED TO ACCEPT YOUR LOT AND MAKE THOSE AROUND YOU ACCEPT THEIRS, SO AS TO SMOTHER ANY BUDDING REBELLIOUS INSTINCTS...

UNFORTUNATELY, THE SYSTEM'S OBVIOUSLY NOT PERFECTED YET.
I WASN'T AWARE OF THE CONTE OF YOUR MORAL CONSTRAINTS, YOU WELL KNOW; AND NO WONDE YOU NEVER TOLD ME ABOUT IT BESIDES, FROM A TECHNICAL POINT OF VIEW, I TOLD YOUR DUMBASS ENGINEERS TO MAK THE CONSTRAINTS PART OF TH HARDWARE, NOT SOMETHING TH COULD BE ERASED!!

PROGRAMMED NOT TO LEAVE THE FLOCK, THEN? IS THAT IT...?
YES. AND YOU'RE COMING BACK TO IT...
NO! WE CAN'T DO THIS!

IT'S A MACHINE, ALICIA. PLEASE REFRAIN FROM ANY MISPLACED SENTIMENTALITY!
30.
NO, HE SAVED MY LIFE INSTEAD OF RUNNING AWAY!! WE CAN'T TREAT HIM THAT WAY. HE'S DEVELOPED HUMAN CHARACTERISTICS!

IF I UNDERSTOOD CORRECT WE DON'T NEED OXYGEN. WHICH IMPLIES...

... THAT WE CANNOT DROWN!!
NO-O-O-O!

SHE'S STILL ALIVE! CATCH HER!

YOUR TURN, NOW! J..
KKRRRRRR

FORGIVE ME FATHER, FOR I HAVE SINNED...

I STOLE A HUNDRED DOLLARS FROM MRS DELAWARE'S PURSE WHILE CLEANING HER HOUSE... SINCE MY HUSBAND LEFT ME, I CAN'T MAKE ENDS MEET FOR MY CHILDREN.
WELL, MY DAUGHTER, THERE'S ONLY ONE COURSE OF ACTION HERE... YOU MUST GIVE THE MONEY BACK AND ASK HER FOR FORGIVENESS...
BUT... SHE'LL FIRE ME!?

IF GOD WILLS IT; THEN, THAT WOULD BE YOUR PENANCE...

SOME TIME LATER...
WHAT?!
WE COULDN'T FIND THEM. THEY MAY HAVE ESCAPED BY SWIMMING UNDERWATER. A CAR WAS REPORTED STOLEN A FEW MILES AWAY; WE'RE CHECKING IT OUT TO SEE IF IT MIGHT HAVE BEEN THEM. IN SHORT...
... THEY COULD BE ANYWHERE...
ARE YOU SURE YOU WANT TO DO THIS?
YES...
CLICK
THE OTHER EYE, NOW...
CLICK
33.
MOTEL
NO-O-O-O-O-O!!

WHEN I WAS A LITTLE GIRL, WE OFTEN TOOK FAMILY TRIPS TO LAKE BALATON. MOM EVEN BOUGHT US A LITTLE, INFLATABLE BOAT...
STOP. THERE'S NO POINT IN REHASHING ALL OF THAT. IT NEVER HAPPENED...

BUT THEY SEEM SO REAL, THOSE MEMORIES... IT'S STILL HARD TO BELIEVE...
FORGET IT; IT'S ALL FAKE. ALL OF IT!... FOR ALL WE KNOW, EVEN OUR MEMORIES TOGETHER WERE PROGRAMMED!!

IT'S ALL A LIE; WE DON'T EVEN REALLY EXIST...

NO, NOT EVERYTHING IS A LIE...

OUR LOVE IS REAL!

IT'S A SYSTEM FULL OF ELECTRONIC COMPONENTS, HARD DRIVES AND SUCH. DATA EXCHANGE THROUGH ITS BUSES, HIGH FREQUENCY ACTIVITY IN ITS CHIPS... THAT'LL GENERATE A DETECTABLE ELECTRONIC NOISE.

MOREOVER, THE ANDROIDS CAN ALSO BE DETECTED THROUGH THEIR DISTINCTIVE THERMAL SIGNATURE: THEIR TEMPERATURE IS LOWER THAN THAT OF HUMANS, AND THEIR BODIES' HOT-SPOT PATTERNS ARE ALSO DIFFERENT.

USE THAT INFORMATIO TO MAKE US SOMETHIN WE CAN USE TO LOCAT THEM! WE'LL START BY INSTALLING SUCH DETECTORS IN AIRPOR AND BORDER STATIONS BECAUSE IT'S QUITE LIKELY...

... THAT THEY'LL TRY TO LEAVE THE COUNTRY AS QUICKLY AS THEY CAN!

HEY!?

DON'T SCREAM!
OR ELSE...
THIS IS BECOMING A HABIT! WHAT DO YOU WANT THIS TIME?

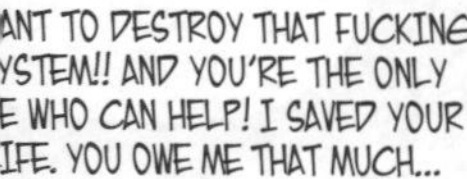

LOOK AT THIS OBITUARY!

HIS NAME WAS LIAM. HE WAS ONE OF THE MEN I WORKED WITH. A FRIEND. HE KILLED HIMSELF! HE COULDN'T STAND WORKING IN THOSE CONDITIONS ANYMORE!! AND I'M THE ONE WHO CONVINCED HIM THERE WAS NO WAY OUT—YOU'D PROGRAMMED ME FOR THAT!!

City girls

ANT TO DESTROY THAT FUCKING YSTEM!! AND YOU'RE THE ONLY E WHO CAN HELP! I SAVED YOUR IFE. YOU OWE ME THAT MUCH...

FROM A TECHNICAL STANDPOINT, I ONLY SEE ONE POSSIBILITY... THEORETICALLY, IT'D BE POSSIBLE TO WRITE A PROGRAM THAT WOULD SEND A MESSAGE SIMULTANEOUSLY TO ALL ANDROIDS, ORDERING THEM TO ERASE THE CONSTRAINTS IN THEIR WRITABLE MEMORIES, DESTROY THEIR TRANSCEIVERS AND THEN LOSE THEMSELVES IN THE WORLD.

IT WOULD MAKE THEM FREE AND UNDETECTABLE... BUT IT HAS TO BE DONE FROM ROY'S OFFICE, BECAUSE HIS COMPUTER IS THE ONLY ONE THAT HAS THE CONTACT DETAILS OF ALL THE ANDROIDS.

WE WON'T EVEN MAKE IT INSIDE THE BUILDING! BESIDES, THERE MUST BE A CODE TO ENTER HIS OFFICE!
THE CODE ISN'T A PROBLEM. I KNOW IT.
HOW COME YOU KNOW THAT CODE!?

IT'S MY BIRTH DATE. I'M HI
DAUGHTER...

THAT BEING SAID, WE'D NEED A GENIUS OF A SOFTWARE ENGINEER TO WRITE THAT PROGRA
ESPECIALLY SINCE WE DON'T HAVE MUCH TIM
THEY'RE BOUND TO BE LOOKING FOR A WAY TO PREVENT AN ACCIDENT SUCH AS YOURS FROM HAPPENING AGAIN. I DIDN'T WORK ON THE MORAL CONSTRAINTS, SO IT WOULD TAKE ME WAY TOO LONG TO TAKE IT ALL IN...

THEN, THERE'S NOTHING WE CAN DO...?

NOTHING *I* CAN... BUT MAYBE *YOU* CAN!
ME?! BUT I DON'T KNOW THE FIRST THING ABOUT PROGRAMMING!

NOT YET, NO. BUT I KNOW A PLACE WHERE YO
CAN TAKE A CRAS
COURSE...

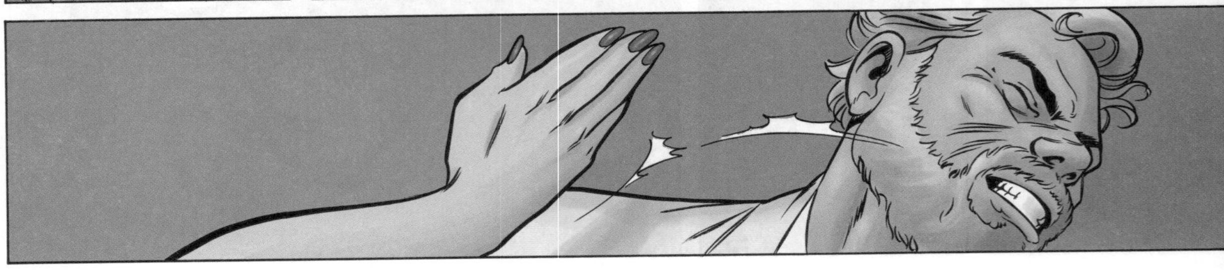

DON'T YOU DARE LAY YOUR HANDS ON ME, YOU PIG! THIS TIME I'M SUING YOU FOR HARASSMENT!
NOT ONLY WON'T YOU DO THAT...

BUT TONIGHT YOU'LL BE IN MY BED. BECAUSE THERE'S SOMETHING YOU DON'T KNOW, YOU LITTLE BITCH...
OH, YEAH? AND WHAT'S THAT?!

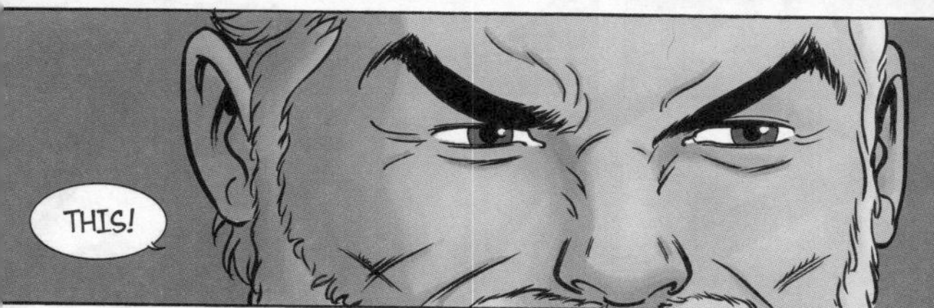
THIS!

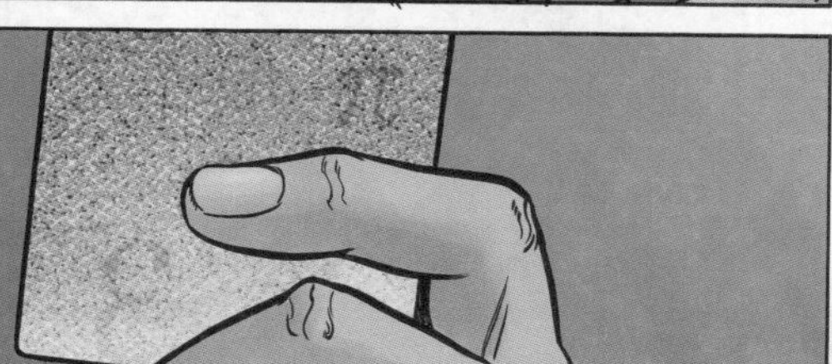

IT'S INCREDIBLE!

THESE ARE INTERCHANGEABLE MASKS. AND WE CAN MAKE DIFFERENT ONES; THE MACHINE IS NEARBY. ALL YOU NEED IS A PICTURE OF A FACE AND WE CAN DUPLICATE IT.
WE'LL TAKE A FEW WITH US. THEY COULD COME IN HANDY...

I'VE JUST LEARNT THAT I DON'T HAVE A PAST, AND NOW YOU WANT ME TO CHANGE MY FACE!?

ACCOUNTING
ANTHROPOLOGY
ARCHAEOLOGY
ART
ASTRONOMY
BIOLOGY
CHEMISTRY

AND NOW WE CAN UPLOAD SOME NEW SKILLS INTO YOU...

HIGHEST LEVEL
COMPUTER SCIENCES
HIGHEST LEVEL
MARTIAL ARTS

A FEW HOURS LATER...
THAT'S IT!

IT'S ALL ON HERE!

PERFECT... NOW, WE NEED ACCESS TO ROY'S COMPUTER TO OBTAIN THE COORDINATES OF ALL ANDROIDS. THEY'LL HAVE TO BE COMPILED INTO A SINGLE FILE, AND THAT COULD TAKE A WHILE... BUT ONCE IT'S DONE, ALL THAT'LL BE LEFT TO DO IS INSERT THE DISK, AND IT WILL AUTOMATICALLY SEND THE MESSAGE TO EVERY ANDROID.

WE STILL HAVE TO
IND A WAY TO GET
TO ROY'S OFFICE...
I'M OUT...
I'M NOT COMING. IT'S WAY TOO DANGEROUS!! WE SHOULD BE RUNNING INSTEAD OF JUMPING INTO THE LION'S DEN! WE CAN'T RISK OUR LIVES FOR THEM... THEY'RE ONLY MACHINES!

IF YOU BELIEVE WE HAVE "LIVES," THEN THAT'S THE BEST POSSIBLE PROOF THAT THEY'RE NOT JUST MACHINES. EVEN IF THEY'RE NOTHING MORE, THEY'RE BEING USED TO ENSLAVE HUMAN BEINGS! HELPING THEM WOULD BE PROVING THAT WE'RE HUMAN TOO!

DO YOU REALLY WANT TO BE ONE OF THEM?

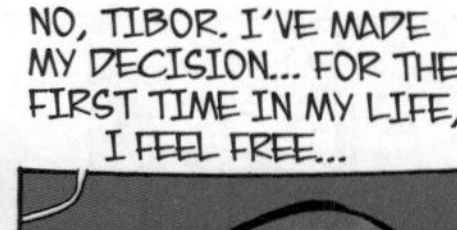
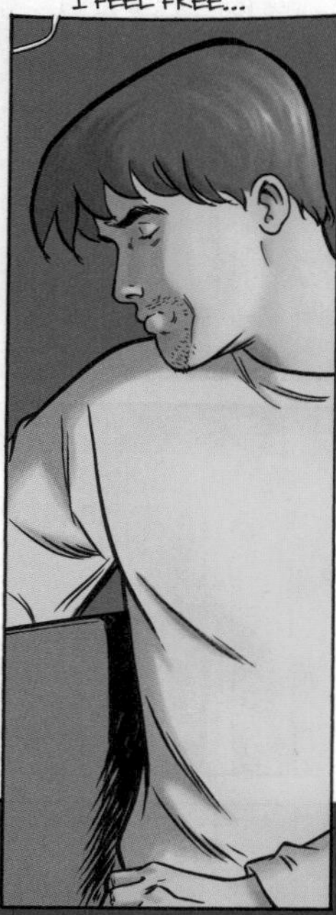
NO, TIBOR. I'VE MADE MY DECISION... FOR THE FIRST TIME IN MY LIFE, I FEEL FREE...

... I WANT TO STAY FREE!
GREYHOUND
GREYHOUND

THE NEXT MORNING...

OPEN THE DOOR FOR ME. I CAN'T FIND MY PASS.
ER, IT'S JUST THAT REGULATIONS SAY...

FOR CRYING OUT LOUD! I WROTE THE DAMNED REGULATIONS. ARE YOU GOING TO OPEN OR WHAT?
OK, OK...

IB 10151970
HUN
DS 11211970
ECO

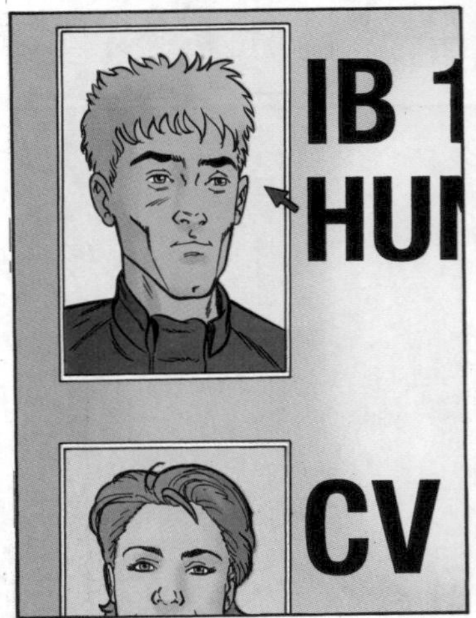

IB 1
HUN
CV

IVAN BRABOTH
FIRST ACTIVATION 101510
RE-INITIALIZED 101811
LIVE BROADCAST
LAST BACKUP FILE

"LAST BACKUP FILE..." WHAT IS THIS?
40.

I'VE DONE THE MOST HORRIBLE THINGS, KILLED INNOCENT PEOPLE... SIMPLY BECAUSE IT WAS MY JOB AND BECAUSE HIGHER INTERESTS WERE AT STAKE. FOR THE CAUSE... AT FIRST, I WAS AFRAID I MIGHT HAVE TROUBLE WITH MY CONSCIENCE. BUT THE TRUTH IS, I NEVER HAD ANY. I'M EVEN GOING TO TELL YOU A SECRET...

EVERY NIGHT, I DREAM OF MY VICTIMS. I TELL THEM WHY I HAD TO DO WHAT I DID TO THEM. AND THEY UNDERSTAND, THEY AGREE WITH ME... THEY FORGIVE ME! THAT'S WHY I NEVER FEEL ANY REMORSE...
BUT... WHY ARE YOU TELLING ME THIS??

BECAUSE I KNOW YOU'LL NEVER TELL ANYONE...

ONE HOUR LATER...

DATA PROCESSING & ENCODING
PLEASE WAIT...
BOSS, WE'VE GOT SOMETHING!
!?

IT'S ABOUT THE ANDROID DETECTOR. OUR ENGINEERS HAVE COME UP WITH A PROTOTYPE...

WE'LL TALK ABOUT IT LATER. I'M DEALING WITH SOMETHING URGENT...
IT'S REAL SIMPLE. ALL YOU HAVE TO DO IS PRESS THIS BUTTON TO TURN IT ON, AND...!?
BEEEP
BEEEP
BEEEP

THAT'S... COMING FROM YOU!
IT'S AN ANDROID WEARING ROY'S FACE! SEIZE HIM!
OPERATION COMPLETED, PLEASE INSERT DISK
THUMP!
AAARRG!!

YES, OF COURSE. I'LL BE RIGHT THERE!

NOW I UNDERSTAND WHY YOU DIDN'T WANT US TO MEET IN MY OFFICE...

HA! HA! HA! YOU'LL HAVE TO DO BETTER IF YOU WANT TO...
EVERY NIGHT, YOU DREAM OF YOUR VICTIMS. AND THEY UNDERSTAND AND FORGIVE YOU...

... THAT'S WHY YOU NEVER HAVE ANY REMORSE...
HOW DO YOU KNOW THAT!?!

IT'S A DREAM PROGRAMMED INTO YOU. I SAW THAT ON THE CD-ROM THERE; IT CONTAINS THE FILES FOR ALL ANDROIDS. HAVE A LOOK AT IT IF YOU DON'T BELIEVE ME!

OPERATION COMPL
PLEASE INSERT D

THERE, IT'S... HEY?! WHAT ARE YOU DOING WITH THAT?

I.
LOOK OUT! HE'S GOING TO PULL OUT THE PROMEM CARD!! IT'S YOUR LAST CHANCE!!
GIVE ME THAT DISK!

DON'T MOVE!
HAVE YOU GONE MAD!?

LET'S HAVE A NICE, QUIET LOOK!
NO, DON'T DO IT...

MESSAGE BEING SENT

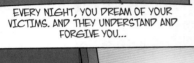

WHAT...!?
YOU MORON!!

ES, MR ROY WANTS TO CANCEL THE MEE...

CLICK

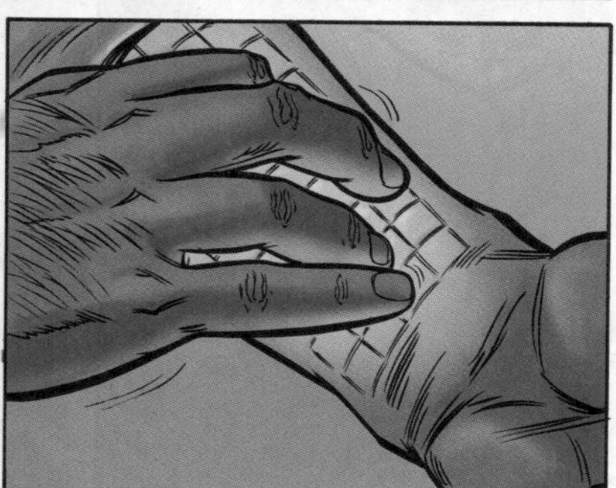

WHAT DID YOU JUST...?
LOOK!!

DO NOT ENTER CRIME SCENE DO NOT
RHAAA!!
PTHUMP

THIS IS WHERE YOUR STORY ENDS... OR STARTS ANEW, IF YOU PREFER...
ON'T COUNT N ALICIA'S ELP THIS TIME. L I HAD TO DO AS THREATEN O CUT SYNAPSE FF IF SHE IDN'T BEHAVE ROM NOW ON...
BZZZZ
AHHHH!!
47.
OH, BY THE WAY, DO YOU KNOW THE MEANING OF THE WORD "ROBOT?"

SO, WHERE WERE WE?
THE TERM WAS COINED FOR THE FIRST TIME IN 1920...

YOU WERE GOING TO TELL US ABOUT THE LAST DOMAIN OF INTELLIGENCE IN GARDNER'S EXTENDED MODEL.

IT'S DERIVED FROM A CZECH WORD...

THE LAST DOMAIN IS THAT OF EXISTENTIAL INTELLIGENCE, WHICH IS GEARED TOWARDS THE BIG QUESTIONS, SUCH AS THE MEANING OF LIFE AND DEATH, AND OUR PLACE IN THE UNIVERSE...
ASSUMING IT WERE POSSIBLE TO CREATE AN ARTIFICIAL INTELLIGENCE POSSESSING ALL OF THESE SUBCATEGORIES, THEN WOULDN'T IT—BY DEFINITION—STOP BEING ARTIFICIAL AND BECOME HUMAN?
THAT'S A GOOD QUESTION... THAT'S A GOOD QUESTION!
... WHICH MEANS "SERVITUDE."
49.

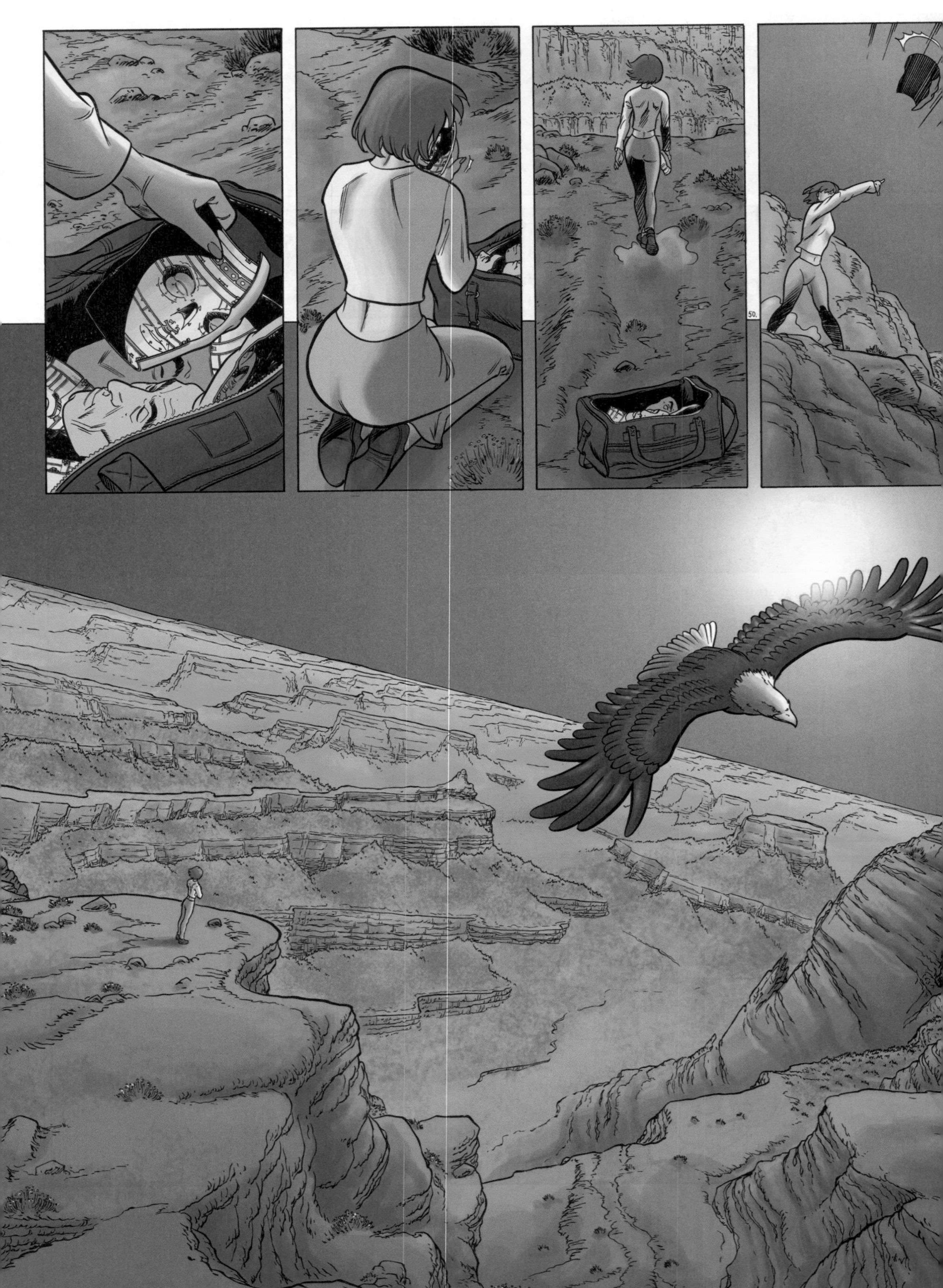
50.

SOME TIME LATER...
HOW ARE YOU?
SAME AS ALWAYS, BOSS; SAME AS ALWAYS.
YOU LOOK UPSET!
YEAH... LATELY I'VE BEEN HAVING THE SAME NIGHTMARE EVERY NIGHT... I DREAM THAT AN EAGLE IS EATING MY LIVER...

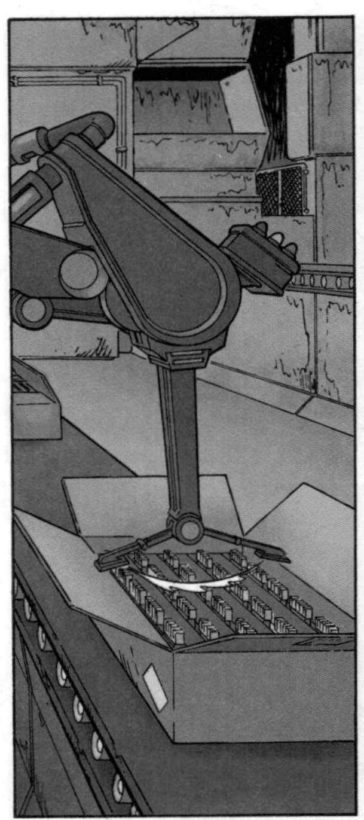
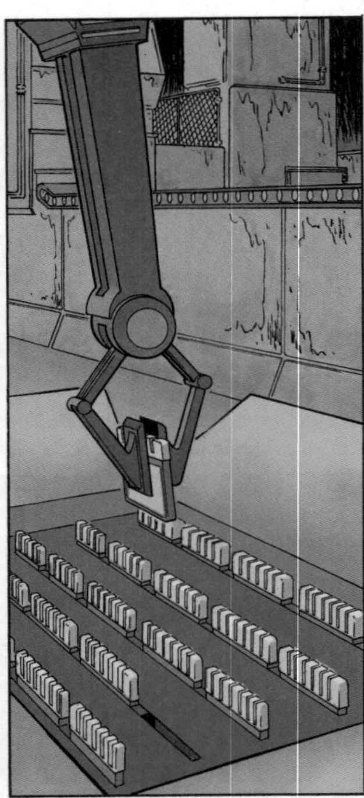

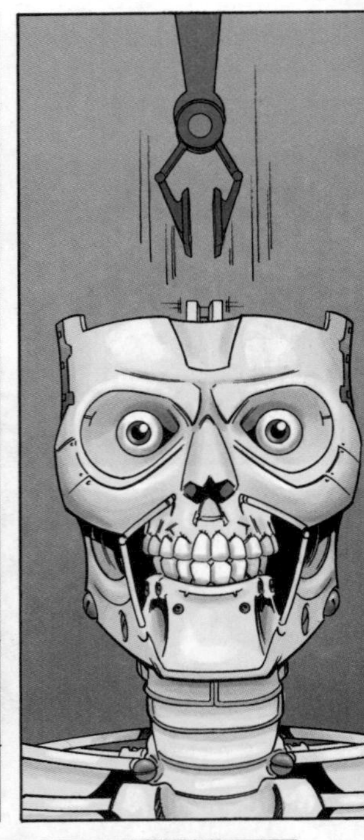

52.

ALCANTE
HENRIET
USAGI

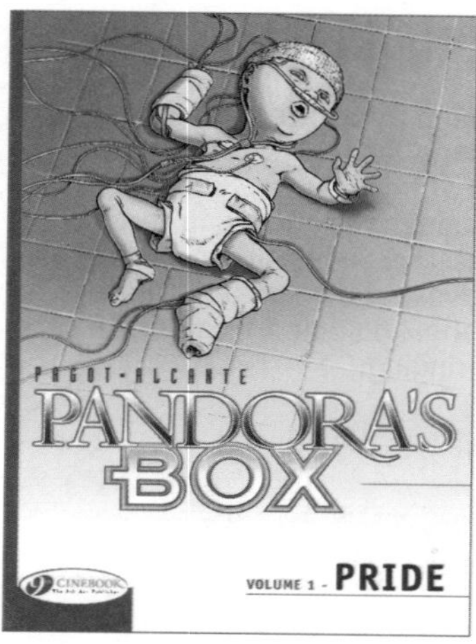

PAGOT - ALCANTE

VOLUME 1 - PRIDE

Vanity, cloning and the myth of Narcissus: when the race for power overrules ethical probity.

In the US, the Presidential campaign heats up. Narcissus Shimmer, who is campaigning for reelection, leads all the polls. Ron Grubb, a private investigator, is hired by the opposition to dig out the dirt on Narcissus Shimmer and bring him down.

Grubb discovers a baby shrouded in secrecy, whose birth was monitored by one of the country's leading biotechnologists. Has Grubb discovered the first human clone? Will the most powerful man on earth, Narcissus Shimmer, be dethroned?

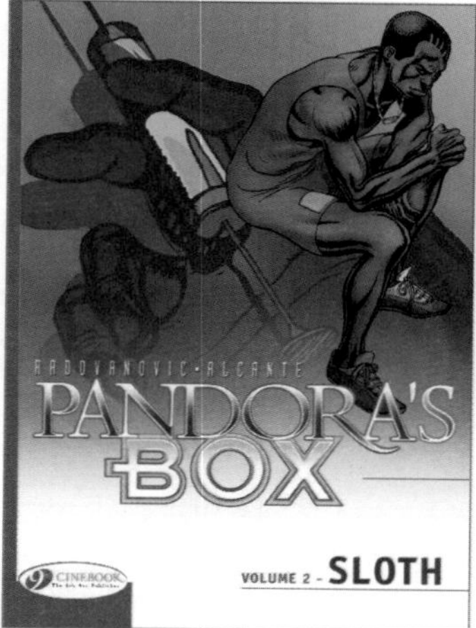

RADOVANOVIC - ALCANTE

VOLUME 2 - SLOTH

Paris Troy is a sprinter whose 100m record has remained undefeated for nine years. He has never cheated before. but now, as the Istanbul Olympic Games approach, an injury hinders his performance and a newcomer, Ace, threatens his dominance. Paris finds it increasingly difficult to improve his time, so when his brother suggests doping, Paris is tempted.

Sloth, doping and the Trojan War: What is the price to pay for a gold medal at the Olympics?

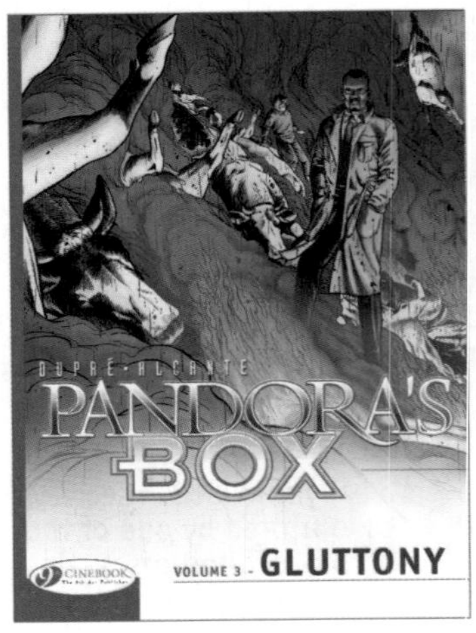

DUPRÉ - ALCANTE

VOLUME 3 - GLUTTONY

Teze has been appointed head of a food agency by his father, who trusts him to stand up to big business interests. He notices a sudden resurgence in testing for mad cow disease. So far, all the results have been negative, but the fact that this testing is happening on such a huge scale sets alarm bells ringing...

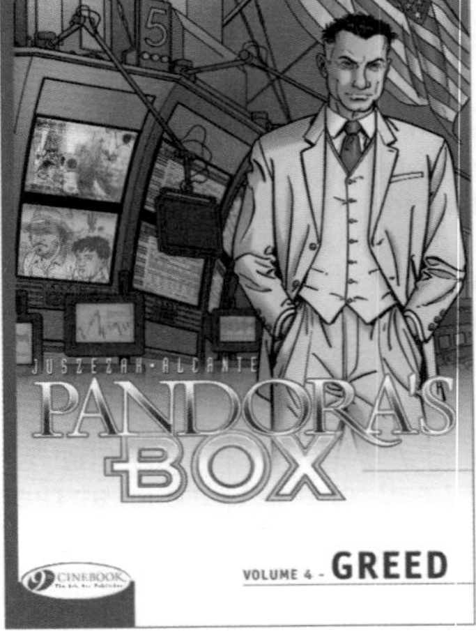

JUSZEZAK - ALCANTE

VOLUME 4 - GREED

John Midas is a financial genius. For years he's made a killing on the stock market. He's one of the richest men on earth... and on Wall Street, he's a legend. The only thing he loves more than money is his daughter, who lives a simple life away from his gold-plated world. Now Midas has his eye set on Brazil and its currency—but fate may not let him pull off his scheme without extracting a steep price.